poetry practice

Brian Keaney and Bill Lucas

Hodder & Stoughton
LONDON SYDNEY AUCKLAND

British Library Cataloguing in Publication Data
Keaney, Brian
　Poetry in Practice
　I. Title II. Lucas, Bill
　808.81

　ISBN 0-340-55168-2

First published 1993

© 1993 Brian Keaney and Bill Lucas

All rights reserved. No part of this publication may be reproduced or transmitted in any form or by any means, electronic or mechanical, including photocopy, recording, or any information storage and retrieval system, without permission in writing from the publisher or under licence from the Copyright Licensing Agency Limited. Further details of such licences (for reprographic reproduction) may be obtained from the Copyright Licensing Agency Limited, of 90 Tottenham Court Road, London W1P 9HE.

Typeset by Wearset, Boldon, Tyne and Wear.
Printed in Great Britain for the educational publishing division of Hodder and Stoughton Ltd, Mill Road, Dunton Green, Sevenoaks, Kent by St Edmundsbury Press, Bury St Edmunds, Suffolk.

Contents

About this anthology

Excuses
The song of the homeworkers	Trevor Millum	7
Excuses	Jamie Hutchins, Sally Kelleher, Stephen Oxley, Grant Smith, Nina Stafford	9
Letter from a Parent	Kenneth Kitchin	12
Not Guilty	Irene Rawnsley	13

The Generation Gap
When I was your age	Michael Frayn	14
Warning	Jenny Joseph	19
When I was 15	Michael Rosen	21
Don't Interrupt!	Demetroulla Vassili	24
Tradition	William Soutar	27

Who Am I?
Two Worlds	Shahana Mirza	28
Snake	D. H. Lawrence	33
'Coward'	Liz Brown	39

Pain into Poetry
Poetry	Shahana Mirza	41
Old Johnny Armstrong	Raymond Wilson	41
Mid-Term Break	Seamus Heaney	43

Earth Matters
The Song of the Whale	Kit Wright	45
Poisoned Talk	Raymond Wilson	47
Who Killed Cock Robin?	Traditional	48
This Letter's to Say	Raymond Wilson	50
The haunted lift	James Kirkup	52
Chipko Andolan	Cath Staincliffe	56

In the Beginning
Noah	Roy Daniells	60
The Sun Witness	Nurunnessa Choudhurry	62

The Shape of Things to Come
A Consumer's Report	Peter Porter	64
'Do you think we'll ever get to see Earth, sir?'	Sheenagh Pugh	66
Evolution Revolution	Andrew Smith	68

The Heart of the Matter
The Moth	Stephen Gardam	80
The Spider	Thea Smiley	82
Riddle	John Mole	84
One question from a bullet	John Agard	85
Raw carrots	Valerie Worth	85

Things Are Not What They Seem
The Sea	James Reeves	86
The Fog	W. H. Davies	88
November Story	Vernon Scannell	89

Relationships
Nobody's Fault	Shahana Mirza	91
Long Distance Phone Call: Michael to Geraldine	Michael Rosen	93
A Poison Tree	William Blake	97

Blue For A Girl
Three Poems for Women	Susan Griffin	100
Interview	Sara Henderson Hay	104
One of the Seven Has Something To Say	Sara Henderson Hay	105
Her Greatest Love	Anna 'Swir'	107
She realised	Anna 'Swir'	107

Beans, Greens and Tangerines
Health Fanatic	John Cooper Clarke	108
about auntie rose & her diet	Jenny Boult	110
Burger Beast	Maria Maryon	112

Shopping
Granny in de Market Place	Amryl Johnson	114
shopping	Jenny Boult	116

The Span of Your Mind
The Door	Miroslav Holub (trans. I. Milner and G. Theiner)	119
The Call	Rachel Mueras	120

The Mysterious Rider
The Way Through the Woods	Rudyard Kipling	122
The Listeners	Walter de la Mare	123
Windy Nights	R. L. Stevenson	124
Bye Now	James Berry	126
Goodbye Now	James Berry	127

About this anthology

There are all sorts of poems in this anthology. There are poems by women, men, young people, established poets and by writers from all sorts of different backgrounds. Some of the poems are long, others are very short indeed. Some are well known, others are published here for the first time. They have all been tried and tested in the classroom, and each one is special in its own particular way.

Most of the poets featured here are modern. They are alive and writing today. We have also included a sprinkling of great writers from the past.

Sometimes we have deliberately put poems in pairs or in groups of three, because we think that this will make them easier to understand, or because it is interesting to see how different writers have dealt with a similar theme.

As well as the poems, there are:

- support materials to help the reader get to grips with the poems;

- activities which are purposeful, relevant and fun;

- illustrations and photographs which have been chosen to highlight the meaning of the poems;

- clear and simple explanations of any technical terms or language features that are necessary for a fuller understanding of the poems.

This book has been compiled with variety in mind. It is organised into sections, each of which deals with a theme which young people will understand and have strong ideas about. Some of these are longer than others – like the poems themselves.

This is also intended to be a practical anthology. There are a whole host of ways of responding to poems and we have tried to present as many of these as possible.

We believe that:

- talking about a poem is as valuable as writing about it;

- there are times when close study of a text is essential;

- an important way of understanding poetry is to write your own.

You will find all of these suggestions included in this book.

Some people think poetry is difficult; others think there is nothing to it. We believe that the truth lies somewhere in the middle. This book is written with the intention of providing assistance where it is required and of letting the poems speak for themselves where it is not.

We hope you enjoy it.

Brian Keaney and Bill Lucas

Excuses

THE SONG OF THE HOMEWORKERS

To be read or chanted with
   increasing velocity

Homework moanwork
Cross it out and groanwork
Homework neatwork
Keeps you off the streetwork
Homework moanwork
Cross it out and groanwork
Homework roughwork
When you've had enoughwork
Homework moanwork
Cross it out and groanwork
Homework dronework
Do it on your ownwork
Homework moanwork
Cross it out and groanwork
Homework gloomwork
Gaze around the roomwork
Homework moanwork
Cross it out and groanwork
Homework guesswork
Book is in a messwork
Homework moanwork
Cross it out and groanwork
Homework rushwork
Do it on the buswork
Homework moanwork
Cross it out and groanwork
Homework hatework
Hand your book in latework
Homework moanwork
Cross it out and groan groan GROANWORK

Trevor Millum

Poetry in practice

Close-up

One reason why this poem is so effective is because of its strong **rhythm**. Rhythm in poetry, like rhythm in music, is the pattern or beat produced by the sounds being made. The main influence on the rhythm of a poem is the number of syllables in each line.

Syllables are the sounds that make up words. For example, the word 'rhythm' is made up of two syllables, or sounds, 'rhyth' and 'm'.

Whether a poem **rhymes** is also important. Rhyming is when the syllables in one word have the same sound as the syllables in another word. For example,

Homework neatwork
Keeps you off the streetwork

Response

The strong rhythm of this poem makes it sound good when chanted out loud.

❖ Write your own 'chant', using rhyme and rhythm to make it fun to read out loud.

Before reading

In groups, tell each other some of the excuses you have used in the past. What is the most outrageously terrible excuse you have ever used with a teacher?

Now read this poem.

EXCUSES

I didn't hand my homework in because
  I forgot it
I didn't hand my homework in because
  I thought I had to hand it in tomorrow
I didn't hand my homework in because
  It blew away on the way to school
I didn't hand my homework in because
  My dog chewed it up

Poetry in practice

I didn't hand my homework in because
  My mum couldn't do it
I didn't hand my homework in because
  I used all the pages to write love letters
  to a tasty bird round the corner
I didn't hand my homework in because
  I put it in the oven instead of my steak
I didn't hand my homework in because
  I ran out of toilet paper and . . .
I didn't hand my homework in because
  The Times Educational Supplement
  wanted to see it first
I didn't hand my homework in because
  You never mark it anyway
I didn't hand my homework in because
  I tripped over a blade of grass
  the book went hurtling through the air
  into a lady's house
  and hit her on the head
  so she tore it up
  and ate it . . .
    . . . honest

Jamie Hutchins, Sally Kelleher, Stephen Oxley,
Grant Smith, Nina Stafford (aged 12)

Response

- Still in groups, write your own 'Excuses' poem. Make it as outrageously amusing as you can. Read it aloud to the rest of the class.

- Both 'Excuses' and 'The song of the homeworkers' on p. 7 have been written in the form of a list. The poets have used this idea to give their subject its particular effect. See how many other poems you can find which have been written in this way.

Poetry in practice

LETTER FROM A PARENT

Dear Sir,

I feel I ought to write
About Toms' essay-work last night.
Of all the subjects you have set
This seemed the most imprudent yet.
'Describe your family'.... Tom did it,
So **well**, I just had to forbid it
Being handed in; — so did my wife.
The details of our family life
Are not of such a kind, alas,
That I should want them read in class:
We did not wish the High School staff
To scan them for a lunch-hour laugh.
We tore it out, I realize
You may think what we did unwise —
But give it your consideration
And please accept my explanation.
I trust you will not blame my son,
For, after all, the work **was done.**

Yours truly
Harold Honeybun

Kenneth Kitchin

First impressions

Do you believe Harold Honeybun? What reasons might he have had for not wanting the school to read about the details of their family life?

Response

❖ Imagine you are the teacher in this poem. Write a letter poem back to Harold Honeybun.

NOT GUILTY

My left boot
keeps kicking people;
when they walk by
it seems to try tripping
them up; I'm always
getting done for it.

My mouth spits paper.
Like cowboys I chew it
then shoot; television
taught me to do it
but Sir blames me
when kids complain.

Excuses come easy
as cartoon bubbles
when I'm in trouble;
what else can I do if
my tongue invents things
that aren't true?

Irene Rawnsley

The generation gap

Poems in Pairs

WHEN I WAS YOUR AGE

When I was your age, child –
When I was eight,
When I was ten,
When I was two
(How old are you?) –
When I was your age, child
My father would have gone quite wild
Had I behaved the way you
Do.
What, food uneaten on my plate
When I was eight?
What, room in such a filthy state
When I was ten?
What, late
For school when I was two?
My father would have shouted, 'When
I was your age, child, my father would have raved
Had I behaved
The way you
Do.'

When I was
Your age, child, I did not drive us
All perpetually mad

By bashing
Up my little brother and reducing him to tears.
There was a war on in those years!
There were no brothers to be had!
Even sisters were on ration!
My goodness, we were pleased
To get anything to tease!
We were glad
Of aunts and dogs and
Of chickens, grandmothers, and frogs;
Of creatures finned and creatures hooved,
And second cousins twice removed!

When I was your
Age, child, I was more
Considerate of others
(Particularly of fathers and of mothers).
I did not sprawl
Reading the Dandy
Or the Beano
When aunts and uncles came to call.
Indeed no.
I grandly
Entertained them all
With 'Please' and 'Thank you,' 'May I . . . ?'
   'Thank you,' 'Sorry,' 'Please,'
And other remarks like these.
And if a chance came in the conversation
I would gracefully recite a line
Which everyone recognised as a quotation
From one of the higher multiplication
Tables, like 'Seven sevens are forty nine.'

Poetry in practice

When I was your age, child, I
Should never have dreamed
Of sitting idly
Watching television half the night.
It would have seemed
Demented:
Television not then having been
Invented.

When I
Was your age, child, I did not lie
About
The house all day.
(I did not lie about anything at all – no Liar I!)
I got out!
I ran away
To sea!
(Though naturally I was back, with hair brushed
   and hands washed, in time for tea.)
Oh yes, goodness me,
When I was nine
I had worked already down a diamond mine,
And fought in several minor wars,
And hunted boars
In the lonelier
Parts of Patagonia
(Though I admit that possibly by then
I was getting on for ten.)
In the goldfields of Australia
I learnt the bitterness of failure;
Experience in the temples of Siam
Made me the wise and punctual man I am;
But the lesson that I value most
I learned upon the Coromandel coast –
Never, come what may, to boast.

The generation gap

When
I was your age, child, and the older generation
Offered now and then
A kindly explanation
Of what the world was like in their young day,
I did not yawn in that rude way.
Why, goodness me,
There being no television to see
(As I have, I think, already said)
We were dashed grateful
For any entertainment we could get instead,
However tedious and hateful.

So grow up, child! And be
Your age! (What is your age, then?
Eight? Or nine? or two? Or ten?)
Remember, as you look at me –
When I was your age I was forty-three.

Michael Frayn

First impressions

Does Michael Frayn expect us to take this poem seriously? What evidence can you find to support your answer?

Close-up

Sometimes, a poet will speak directly to the reader through a poem. Sometimes, however, a poem is written as if from someone else's point of view. Which is happening in 'When I was your age'?

We call the person 'speaking' a poem the **narrator**. Why do you think, if a poet disagrees with what his or her narrator is saying, he or she does not tell the reader so directly? Do you think Michael Frayn agrees with the narrator here?

Before reading

What are your immediate reactions when someone mentions 'old people'? In groups, decide

- how many old people you know;
- how many old people you know *well*;
- if all old people are the same;
- what the problems are of growing old;
- if you can think of any advantages connected with growing old.

WARNING

When I am an old woman I shall wear purple
With a red hat which doesn't go, and doesn't suit me,
And I shall spend my pension on brandy and summer gloves
And satin sandals, and say we've no money for butter.
I shall sit down on the pavement when I'm tired
And gobble up samples in shops and press alarm bells
And run my stick along the public railings
And make up for the sobriety of my youth.
I shall go out in my slippers in the rain
And pick the flowers in other people's gardens
And learn to spit.

You can wear terrible shirts and grow more fat
And eat three pounds of sausages at a go
Or only bread and pickle for a week
And hoard pens and pencils and beermats and things in boxes.

But now we must have clothes that keep us dry
And pay the rent and not swear in the street
And set a good example for the children.
We must have friends to dinner and read the papers.

But maybe I ought to practise a little now?
So people who know me are not too shocked and surprised
When suddenly I am old and start to wear purple.

Jenny Joseph

Poetry in practice

Close-up

- What sort of old woman does Jenny Joseph intend to become? Why do you think she wants to end up like this?

- In the second verse of the poem, Jenny Joseph talks about how she feels old people are allowed to behave. In the third verse she describes the way *she* has to behave 'now'. How old do you think she is 'now'? At what age does she think people have most freedom? Do you agree with her?

Response

❖ Both these poems are about how you are expected to behave at a certain age. Write your own poem about acting your age.

Before you begin

- Think about how other people expect you to behave: family, friends, enemies, teachers, strangers and anyone else you can think of.

- Think about the way they behave towards you. Do *they* always act their age?

- Think of what you would like to say to these people about how they treat you, if you had the chance.

WHEN I WAS 15

Ken said to me,
'You know your trouble,
you don't hold your bag right.'
'What's wrong with it?' I said.
5 'It's not so much the way you hold it –
It's the way you put it down.
You've got to look at it as if you hate it.
Watch me.'

He went out
10 he walked back in
shoulders back
elbows out
bag balanced in his hand.

'Watch me.'

15 He stopped walking.
His arm froze
and the bag flew out of his hand
as if he'd kicked it.
He didn't even look at it.

Poetry in practice

20 'Now you try,' he said.
    'I'll show you where you've gone wrong.'
    I went out the door,
    I rambled back in again with my bag.
    I stopped walking
25 My arm froze – just like his,
    but the bag fell out of my hand
    and flopped on to the floor
    like a fried egg.

    'Useless,' he said.
30 'You don't convince – that's your trouble.'
    'So?' I said.
    'I'm a slob. I can't change that.'

    I didn't say that I *would* try and change
    in case that would show I was giving in to him.
35 But secretly
    on my own,
    in my room,
    in front of the mirror
    I spent hours and hours
40 practising bag-dropping.
    Walking in,
    freeze the arm,
    let the bag drop.
    Walk in
45 arm freeze
    bag drop.
    Again and again
    till I thought I had got it right.

    I don't suppose any girl noticed.
50 I don't suppose any girl ever said to herself,
    'I love the way he drops his bag . . .'

                                    Michael Rosen

First impressions

In pairs, look at this list of statements about the poem. Which of them do you agree with and which do you disagree with? Add some of your own statements about the poem.

'When I Was 15' is a poem about:

- a boy called Ken;
- how much the author hated school;
- a teenage boy trying to impress girls;
- bullying;
- friendship;
- a teenage boy trying to look cool.

What can you find out about the relationship between the two boys? Use these questions to help you:

- What sort of person do you think Ken is?
- Why does the narrator take so much notice of him?
- What sort of person do you think the narrator is?
- What sort of person does he want to be?

Look especially at lines 32–4.

Response

- In pairs, act out the poem and prepare a performance for the rest of the class.
- Make up your own poem, suitable for performing to the rest of the class, about a boy or girl who gets advice from a friend.

Before you begin

- Think about your characters. How old are they? Where are they? What are their likes and dislikes? What are their problems?

- Think about their relationship. Try to make it like the one in the poem. One of them should be

Poetry in practice

very unsure of himself or herself. What reasons could he or she have? The other one should think he or she knows best.

- What is the advice about? School? Clothes? The opposite sex? Music? Sport? Getting out of trouble? Is the advice helpful?

Before reading

One of the things that young people most often complain about is nagging parents. In your groups, answer these questions:

- Do you suffer from nagging?
- Why do you think people nag?
- What sort of things do they say?
- What do you say in reply?
- Do parents need to be nagged?

DON'T INTERRUPT!

Turn the television down!
None of your cheek!
Sit down!
Shut up!
Don't make a fool of yourself!
Respect your elders!
I can't put up with you anymore!
Go outside.
Don't walk so fast!
Don't run.
Don't forget to brush your teeth!
Don't forget to polish your shoes!
Don't slam the door!
Have manners!
Don't interrupt when I'm talking!
Put your hand over your mouth when you cough.

● The generation gap

Poetry in practice

Don't talk with your mouth full!
Go to the market with me.
You spend too much money!
No more pocket money for you dear.
Go to your room!
Don't stuff yourself with sweets!
Don't point!
Don't go too near the television.
You are not coming out until you have tidied your room.
Don't interrupt when I'm talking!
Did you get any homework today?
Always carry a pen to school.
Eat your dinner up.
Wear your school uniform!
Turn the television over to watch 'Dallas'.
Bring any letters home from school.
Come straight home tomorrow.
Tidy your bed.
Don't shout!
Don't listen to my conversation.
Don't look at the sun it could blind you.
Don't bite your nails!
Don't suck your thumb!
Why don't you answer me!
You never listen to a word I say!
Don't interrupt when I'm talking.

Demetroulla Vassili

Close-up

- This poem is made up of a list of orders. One of them, 'Don't interrupt when I'm talking' is repeated three times. Why do you think the poet does this?

- 'Why don't you answer me?' the narrator demands. Why don't we hear anything from the person who is being ordered about?

TRADITION

'Heh! young folk arena what they were:'
Wheeng'd the auld craw to his cronie:
'Sic galivantin' here and there,
Sic wastrie and aye wantin' mair;
Their menners far frae bonnie.

'Eh me! it's waur and waur they get
In gumption and decorum:
And sma' respec' for kirk or state.'
Wi' that the auld craw wagg'd his pate
As his faither did afore him.

William Soutar

First impressions

This poem is written in a Scottish dialect. In groups, read it out loud and see how much of it you can understand.

Close-up

What is the point of the last line? Would the poem have the same meaning without it? Why do you think the poet chose the title, 'Tradition'?

Who am I?

Before reading

In groups, find out where each of you was born. Were your parents born in the same place?
   What do you know about your parents' childhoods? In what ways were they different from yours?

TWO WORLDS

I live in two worlds.
I have two names.
I have two ways of dressing
And two languages.

When I'm out there,
I want to be like them,
Moaning about boyfriends
And high street fashions.

But inside my mind
I long for the warmth of home,
The warmth of heaters turned up
On summer days
And the climbing flowered wall paper
In crowded rooms.
Or the furniture
Which was never quite in fashion.

Sometimes the outside world
Comes to visit us.
Then the new table cloths,
Our best cutlery
And our politest smiles
Welcome them.

They never see our real world, though.
It is hidden in cupboards,
Behind curtains,
And underneath the beds.

Then we put on our best clothes
And we eat mildly spiced curries
With a knife and fork
And speak their language
Because they do not speak ours.

When I leave
And set up my own place,
I wonder if I'll have
Heaters turned up on summer days
And climbing flowered wallpaper?

Or will I eat mildly spiced curries
With a knife and fork,
And speak their language
Because I do not speak ours?

Shahana Mirza

SHAHANA MIRZA

I'm sort of somewhere in the middle, I suppose. I don't speak my language as well as I should.

How old were you when you wrote 'Two Worlds'?
Probably about seventeen or eighteen.

And where were you living?
I was living in Leeds with my parents.

Looking back on it now, seven years later, was it really like your life at the time?
I didn't actually write it because I wanted to write a poem but because I felt really strongly about something. So when I wrote it, it was exactly what I was feeling and it turned into a poem afterwards because I found that it was making its own rhythm.

'Two Worlds' seems to be about your own world and your parents' world. Why were they different?
Well, obviously, I was born in Leeds, but my parents came from Pakistan.

Would you say that your parents expected you to stay in England or at some point to go and live in Pakistan?
They never expected me to live in Pakistan.

So they always saw you as being British?
Yes.

Does this ever cause any conflict between you?
I'm sure it does. It's difficult to pinpoint where exactly the conflict is. It can be something really little, for example my parents being irritated by the fact that when I was younger I always used to go straight home and change into traditional clothes and then as soon as I was going out, even if I was only going to the corner shop, I would change back into trousers.

So you're saying that when you were at school you wore Western clothes? You put on traditional clothes when you came home, but when you went out again you changed back into Western clothes?
Yeah, I just didn't feel comfortable going out in traditional clothes.

Why was that?
Because of the way people reacted. Even now if I'm wearing traditional clothes and I go out shopping, I get a different feeling about how people respond to me. Sometimes they're taken aback when I start to speak because I look very Asian when I wear traditional clothes and they don't expect the English accent.

At the end of your poem 'Two Worlds', you wonder how things will turn out and who you feel you will be in the future. Have you answered that question? How have you turned out?
I think I'm somewhere in between. I thought that maybe when I was older I'd forget about my own culture, and I haven't done. And yet I must admit I do eat mildly spiced curries now, more mildly spiced than I used to, simply because if I'm cooking for friends who aren't Asian, it doesn't make sense to make them really spicy. So I'm sort of somewhere in the middle, I suppose. I don't speak my language as well as I should.

Do you think of yourself as a poet?
No.

But yet you write poetry?
Yes.

Why's that then?
I think of myself as someone who's got something to say, and the reason I like to write poetry is that I know that people out there are going to identify with that.

What do you think it is that you're writing about, in a nutshell?
I'm writing about what it's like to be me. I'm aware that there are lots of people like me. I didn't know that when I was young.

Poetry in practice

Close-up

- Shahana Mirza talks about living in two worlds. What do you think these are? Which words used in the poem do you associate with each of these worlds? Make two lists, and give a title to each.
- Look at the interview with Shahana Mirza on pages 30–1, then reread the poem. Which particular lines in the poem are made clearer by the interview?

Response

Most people live in more than one 'world' and are influenced by different people. These may include friends, enemies, parents, brothers, sisters, teachers and many others.

❖ Take it in turns to tape-record an interview with a friend about growing-up, especially about those things or people that have had a strong influence on him or her.

Before you begin

- Think about the kind of questions you will ask. They should encourage your friend to talk in detail. You might find it helpful to look at the kind of questions we asked Shahana Mirza.
- Make a list of your questions.
- Remember, you should also be ready to ask extra questions during the interview, to help you find out more about what your friend tells you.

❖ Write your own poem called 'Two Worlds'.

Before you begin

- Listen to the interview that your friend has conducted with you. Think about the answers you gave to his or her questions.

- Reread Shahana Mirza's poem. Some of the verses deal with the world outside her home, some with the world inside. You might like to organise your poem in a similar way. You might also like to use the same first line or lines.

Before reading

What do you think of snakes? What would you do if you found one? In groups, make a list of all the words that you associate with a snake.

SNAKE

A snake came to my water-trough
On a hot, hot day, and I in pyjamas for the heat,
To drink there.

In the deep, strange-scented shade of the great dark carob-tree
5 I came down the steps with my pitcher
And must wait, must stand and wait, for there he was at the trough before me.

He reached down from a fissure in the earth-wall in the gloom
And trailed his yellow-brown slackness soft-bellied down, over
10   the edge of the stone trough
And rested his throat upon the stone bottom,
And where the water had dripped from the tap, in a small clearness,
He sipped with his straight mouth,
15 Softly drank through his straight gums, into his slack long body,
Silently.

Someone was before me at my water-trough,
And I, like the second comer, waiting.

He lifted his head from his drinking, as cattle do,
20 And looked at me vaguely, as drinking cattle do,
And flickered his two-forked tongue from his lips, and mused a moment,
And stooped and drank a little more,

Being earth-brown, earth-golden from the burning bowels of the earth
On the day of Sicilian July, with Etna smoking.

The voice of my education said to me
He must be killed,
For in Sicily the black, black snakes are innocent, the gold are venomous.
And voices in me said, If you were a man
You would take a stick and break him now, and finish him off.

But must I confess how I liked him,
How glad I was he had come like a guest in quiet, to drink at my water-trough
And depart peaceful, pacified, and thankless,
Into the burning bowels of this earth?

Was it cowardice, that I dared not kill him?
Was it perversity, that I longed to talk to him?
Was it humility, to feel so honoured?
I felt so honoured.

And yet those voices:
If you were not afraid, you would kill him!

And truly I was afraid, I was most afraid,
But even so, honoured still more
That he should seek my hospitality
From out the dark door of the secret earth.

He drank enough
And lifted his head, dreamily, as one who has drunken,
And flickered his tongue, like a forked night on the air, so black,
Seeming to lick his lips,
And looked around like a god, unseeing, into the air,
And slowly turned his head,
And slowly, very slowly, as if thrice adream,
Proceeded to draw his slow length curving round
And climb again the broken bank of my wall-face.

And he put his head into that dreadful hole,
And as he slowly drew up, snake-easing his shoulders, and entered farther,
A sort of horror, a sort of protest against his withdrawing into that horrid black hole,

Deliberately going into the blackness, and slowly drawing
   himself after,
Overcame me now his back was turned.

65 I looked round, I put down my pitcher,
I picked up a clumsy log
And threw it at the water-trough with a clatter.

I think it did not hit him,
But suddenly that part of him that was left behind convulsed in
70   undignified haste,
Writhed like lightning, and was gone
Into the black hole, the earth-lipped fissure in the wall-front,
At which, in the intense still noon, I stared with fascination.

And immediately I regretted it.
75 I thought how paltry, how vulgar, what a mean act!
I despised myself and the voices of my accursed human
   education.

And I thought of the albatross,
And I wished he would come back, my snake.

80 For he seemed to me again like a king,
Like a king in exile, uncrowned in the underworld,
Now due to be crowned again.

And so, I missed my chance with one of the lords
Of life.
85 And I have something to expiate;
A pettiness.

D. H. Lawrence

Poetry in practice

First impressions

- Without worrying too much about whether you understand the more difficult words in 'Snake', what do you think the narrator felt towards the creature at

• the start;

• the middle;

• the end of the poem?

❖ Choose five of the words which Lawrence uses to describe the snake which you found the most effective on first reading the poem. How do the words Lawrence uses to describe the snake compare with the list you made earlier? Which word or words do you think best sums up how the narrator felt at the end of the poem? Has this poem made you think differently about snakes in any way?

Close-up

Look at any of the words that you found difficult to understand in 'Snake'.

The more you read this poem, the more you will see how the poet has used particular ways of bringing the snake alive on the page.

In lines 14–16, listen to the way the sound of the letter 's' is repeated. When the same sound is repeated at the beginning of a series of words, it is called **alliteration**. How do you think this particular technique adds to your picture of the snake?

In line 52, Lawrence describes the snake as being 'like a god'. The snake is not a god, of course, but to the poet it seems for a moment to be one. Comparing one thing with something else in this way, normally with the words 'like' or 'as', is called using a **simile**. A simile helps the reader understand the appearance or behaviour of a person, object or event more clearly. In this case, the simile helps us to see the snake in a new light. What other similies does Lawrence use in this poem and what do they add to our understanding of this picture of a man and a snake?

The narrator's reaction to seeing the snake is quite complicated. Reread lines 27–8, 31–2 and 76. What are the voices saying and where do they come from? What do the narrator's feelings tell him he should do? Why does he end up throwing a log at the snake?

Poetry in practice

Response

'Snake' is written as if the reader were inside the narrator's head or as if the poet were talking to himself. By now you will have realised how his thoughts and feelings change as he watches the snake.

❖ Imagine you are the narrator. You have just seen the snake disappear into the hole in the wall. It is very hot. You have left your house and wandered into the village to get yourself some lunch in the shade.

Imagine now that you are writing to a friend and telling him or her about your encounter with the snake. Use each verse of the poem to help you describe the various different thoughts, emotions and feelings you have experienced.

Before reading

In groups, look at this series of statements. Say which you agree with and which you disagree with. Give your reasons.

- All war is wrong.
- All killing is murder.
- Killing in self-defence is justified.
- Everyone who joins an army should expect to have to kill.
- A soldier who will not kill is a coward.
- A soldier who will not kill is brave.
- People don't know what they are letting themselves in for when they join an army.
- Killing can be right in certain situations.
- Suicide is wrong.
- Every person has the right to take his or her own life.
- People should be prepared to fight for their own country.

Who am I?

'COWARD'

Here lies the soldier they called 'coward' –
a pacifist by nature.
He had said all along –
'I shall not kill!' he'd said.
But he had to be bluffing,
there was a war on, after all!
And sure enough,
when faced with that bloody enemy,
he took up his gun,
pulled back the trigger,
and then, with menacing eyes,
    he shot –
           himself –
                  dead.
Here lies that soldier.
They called him 'coward'.

Liz Brown (aged 16)

Poetry in practice

Close-up

A poem like this is called an **epitaph**. An epitaph is a poem written about a person who has died. Many epitaphs are written on tombstones, and begin with the words, 'Here lies . . .'

The writer of an epitaph often uses it as a way of summing up the dead person's life. What do you think that Liz Brown thinks of the dead soldier? Does she think that he was a coward or not? Give your reasons. Do you agree?

Pain into poetry

POETRY

She liked the park, except when the
Big kids said words to her. Words that
She didn't really understand
But she could feel the sound of them.

Hot and sharp, like a hard slap
And then she'd go red all over
And feel like crying and running
Home. But home was too far away.

So she'd find an empty corner
And there she'd sit, alone with her
Thoughts. Thinking one day she'd find the
Words to tell them how she felt.

Shahana Mirza

OLD JOHNNY ARMSTRONG

Old Johnny Armstrong's eighty or more
And he humps like a question-mark
Over two gnarled sticks as he shuffles and picks
His slow way to Benwell Park.

He's lived in Benwell his whole life long
And remembers how street-lights came,
And how once on a time they laid a tram-line,
Then years later dug up the same!

Now he's got to take a lift to his flat,
Up where the tall winds blow
Round a Council Block that rears like a rock
From seas of swirled traffic below.

Old Johnny Armstrong lives out his life
In his cell on the seventeenth floor,
And it's seldom a neighbour will do him a favour
Or anyone knock at his door.

Poetry in practice

With his poor hands knotted with rheumatism
And his poor back doubled in pain,
Why, day after day, should he pick his slow way
To Benwell Park yet again? –

*O the wind in park trees is the self-same wind
That first blew on a village child
When life freshly unfurled in a green, lost world
And his straight limbs ran wild.*

Raymond Wilson

Close-up

Looking hard at the end of the poem can sometimes help you to understand more about the whole poem.

'Old Johnny Armstrong' ends quite surprisingly. In pairs, look closely at the last four lines and decide:

- what you think they mean;

- what they tell us about Johnny Armstrong.

Response

❖ Imagine you are a reporter on a local newspaper and that you are to write a feature about an old man, Old Johnny Armstrong, who lives on the seventeenth floor of a block of flats but who still goes to visit the park every day. Part of your job will be to interview this man.

Before you begin

Prepare a list of questions you will ask him based

- on the information in the poem;
- on what your readers would like to know.

MID-TERM BREAK

I sat all morning in the college sick bay
Counting bells knelling classes to a close.
At two o'clock our neighbours drove me home.

In the porch I met my father crying –
he had always taken funerals in his stride –
And Big Jim Evans saying it was a hard blow.

The baby cooed and laughed and rocked the pram
When I came in, and I was embarrassed
By old men standing up to shake my hand

And tell me they were 'sorry for my trouble',
Whispers informed strangers I was the eldest,
Away at school, as my mother held my hand

In hers and coughed out angry tearless sighs.
At ten o'clock the ambulance arrived
With the corpse, stanched and bandaged by the
    nurses.

Next morning I went up into the room. Snowdrops
And candles soothed the bedside; I saw him
For the first time in six weeks. Paler now,

Wearing a poppy bruise on his left temple,
He lay in the four foot box as in his cot.
No gaudy scars, the bumper knocked him clear.

A four foot box, a foot for every year.

Seamus Heaney

Earth matters

THE SONG OF THE WHALE

Heaving mountain in the sea,
Whale, I heard you
Grieving.

Great whale, crying for your life,
Crying for your kind, I knew
How we would use
Your dying:

> LIPSTICK FOR OUR PAINTED FACES,
> POLISH FOR OUR SHOES.

Tumbling mountain in the sea,
Whale, I heard you
Calling.

Bird-high notes, keening, soaring:
At their edge a tiny drum
Like a heart-beat.

We would make you
Dumb.

In the forest of the sea,
Whale, I heard you
Singing,

Singing to your kind.
We'll never let you be.
Instead of life we choose

> LIPSTICK FOR OUR PAINTED FACES,
> POLISH FOR OUR SHOES.

Kit Wright

First impressions

Which line or lines in this poem made the most impact on you? What was it about it (or them) which you were particularly impressed by?

Close-up

- Why do you think Kit Wright chooses to include each of these words in a poem about a whale: Song, Crying, Bird-high, PAINTED? What do you normally associate with these words?

- Kit Wright uses a simile in the middle of this poem. (If you are uncertain what a simile is, look back to the explanation on p. 37.) Why do you think he chooses to make this comparison? Do you think it is an effective one?

Response

- Write your own poem about a creature of your choice which you think is in some danger from the human race.

Before you begin

- Think about your particular creature and how its life is affected by human beings.

- If your creature were to sing, what sort of voice might it have? What might it sing about and what words might be particularly important to it? Decide what type of song it might sing.

Poems in Pairs

Before reading

Ask yourself whether the first line of this poem reminds you of anything you have heard or read before.

POISONED TALK

Who killed cock robin?
I, said the worm,
I did him great harm.
He died on the branch of a withered tree
From the acid soil that poisoned me.

Who killed the heron?
I, mouthed the fish,
With my tainted flesh
I killed tern, duck and drake,
All the birds of the lake.

Who killed the lake?
I, boasted Industry,
I poisoned with mercury
Fish, plant and weed
To pamper man's greed.

Who killed the flowers?
I, moaned the wind,
I prowl unconfined,
Blowing acid rain
Over field, flood and fen.

Who killed the forest?
I ensured that it died,
Said sulphur dioxide,
And all life within it,
From earthworm to linnet.

Raymond Wilson

First impressions

What message do you think Raymond Wilson is trying to put across in 'Poisoned Talk'? You may find it helpful to look closely at each verse in turn.

Close-up

In fact, this poem is a **parody**. A parody is an imitation of another piece of writing. It is usually written to make a point, sometimes a funny one, or, as in this case, a more serious one and it does so by mocking or making fun of what the original writer had to say.

'Poisoned Talk' is a parody of a nursery rhyme called 'Who Killed Cock Robin?'. To help you understand 'Poisoned Talk', read the original nursery rhyme and compare it with the parody.

WHO KILLED COCK ROBIN?

Who killed Cock Robin?
I, said the sparrow,
With my bow and arrow
I killed Cock Robin.

Who saw him die?
I, said the fly,
With my little eye,
I saw him die.

Who caught his blood?
I, said the fish,
With my little dish, I caught his blood.

Who will make his shroud?
I, said the beetle,
With my thread and needle,
I'll make his shroud.

Who'll dig his grave?
I, said the owl,
With my pick and shovel,
I'll dig his grave.

Traditional

Close-up

- In pairs, make a list of all the ways in which these two poems are similar to each other. Make a note of any words you did not understand.
   Which of the two poems did you find it easier to understand? What do you think the poet in that particular poem is trying to say?

- Look up the meaning of the words you did not know, and then read the poems out loud. Does reading them out loud make any difference in helping you to work out what the poet is trying to say?

Response

- Choose a subject that concerns you. It might be to do with the environment or it might be another topic about which you feel strongly.
   Write your own parody in which you try to put across your point of view. You could base it on the form of 'Who Killed Cock Robin?' or on another song or nursery rhyme of your own choice.

Before you begin

- Study the way in which the original poem is written. This will help you to parody it. For example, decide how many lines there are in each verse, whether it rhymes or not, if there is a repeated pattern (as in the first line of each verse in 'Who Killed Cock Robin?').

- Be clear about the message you wish to put across.

Poetry in practice

Poems in Pairs

THIS LETTER'S TO SAY

Dear Sir or Madam,
This letter's to say
Your property
Stands bang in the way
Of Progress, and
Will be knocked down
On March the third
At half-past one.

There is no appeal,
Since the National Need
Depends on more
And still more Speed
And this, in turn,
Dear Sir or Madam,
Depends on half England
Being tar-macadam.
(But your house will –
We are pleased to say –
Be the fastest lane
Of the Motorway).

Meanwhile the Borough
Corporation
Offer you new
Accomodation
Three miles away
On the thirteenth floor
(Flat Number Q
6824).

But please take note,
The Council regret:
No dog, cat, bird
Or other pet;
No noise permitted,
No singing in the bath,
(For permits to drink
Or smoke or laugh
Apply on Form
Z 327);
No children admitted
Aged under eleven;
No hawkers, tramps
Or roof-top lunchers;
No opening doors
To Bible-punchers.
Failure to pay
Your rent, when due,
Will lead to our
Evicting you.
The Council demand
That you consent
To the terms above
When you pay your rent.
Meanwhile we hope
You will feel free
To consult us
Should there prove to be
The slightest case
Of difficulty.

With kind regards,
Yours faithfully . . .

Raymond Wilson

Poetry in practice

THE HAUNTED LIFT

On the ground floor
of this ultramodern
tower block

in the dead
middle
of the night

the lift doors
open, with a
clang.

Nobody enters,
and nobody
comes out.

In the dead
middle
of the night

the lift doors
close with a clang,
and the lift begins

to move
slowly
up –

with nobody in it,
nobody but
the ghost of a girl

who lived here once
on the thirteenth floor of
this ultramodern tower block.

One day, she went to play
in an old part of town,
and never came back.

She said she was just
going to the corner shop,
but she never came home.

Now her ghost
keeps pressing
in the dead

middle of the night
the button
for the thirteenth floor.

But when the door
opens with a clang
she cannot step out.

She gazes longingly
at the familiar landing,
but only for a moment –

then the lift doors
clang in her face
and her tears

silently flow
as the lift
in the dead

middle
of the night
so soft and slow

carries her down again
down below,
far, far below

the ground
floor, where nobody
waits for the haunted lift

in the dead
middle
of the night.

Sometimes
on the thirteenth floor
her mother and father

with her photo
beside their bed
wake up

in the dead
middle of the night, and hear
the mysterious clanging

Poetry in practice

of closing lift doors,
and wonder
who it could be

in the dead
middle
of the night

using the lift
at such
an unearthly hour.

– In this ultramodern
tower block
there is no thirteenth floor.

James Kirkup

First impressions

What do you think these two poems have in common? Which one do you prefer? Why do you think this is?

Close-up

- In both of these poems it is possible to work out the poet's opinion of the area in which the people he is describing live. In groups, decide what Raymond Wilson and James Kirkup really think about the situations they describe.

Response

❖ Write a letter poem of your own concerning something you feel strongly about.

Before you begin

Decide who you are writing to and what point you are trying to make.

❖ In groups, imagine you are a TV news crew and that you are going to make a report based on one of the poems you have just read.

Before you begin

• Decide who you want to interview. For example, for 'The Haunted Lift' you might want to talk to the parents, someone from the corner shop or someone from the local council.

• Decide who is going to be the interviewer and who are going to be interviewees.

• Agree on a list of questions and what the answers will be. It will help to write them down in note form.

• Practise asking and answering the questions a few times until you no longer need to look at your notes. Remember, you don't have to be word perfect; you are trying to look natural.

• Either tape-record or video your interview.

Poetry in practice

CHIPKO ANDOLAN

She hugs the tree
Skin against bark
No wind stirs its canopy
The tree is listening.
In the distance
The whine of machinery
The drone of a generator.

She hugs the tree
Her form a bright dab
Of colour at the bottom
Of the old – old trunk.
The patterns of the bark
Echoed in the network of lines
Around her knuckles
Across her strong hands.

She knows
This tree has to be saved
She understands
The balance.
The way life supports life
And death breeds death.
She sees –
The trees bind the earth
The trees hold up the sky

She and her sisters
A hundred strong
Hug the trees
Till chainsaws fall silent
A muttered retreat,
Peals of laughter
Ring through the glades.

We have won.
We hugged the trees.
We saved the forest.

Cath Staincliffe

Response

❖ 'Chipko Andolan' is the story of how villagers in India saved their local forest. Retell the story of the poem from the point of view of one of the villagers.

Before you begin

Read the Back-Up File on p. 58 for more information on what actually happened.

CHIPKO ANDOLAN: THE FACTS

Chipko Andolan means 'the movement to hug' in Hindi. The organisation was born in north-east India in 1973. For centuries the local population of Gopeshwar, a remote hill-town close to the border with Tibet, had relied on forest products for food, shelter, raw materials, medicines and fodder for their animals. Then the government sold a licence to cut down trees to a manufacturer of sporting goods.

Local people were told they could no longer go into the forest. The company sent loggers to cut down ten ash trees. The villagers decided to resist the loggers. There is an old Indian legend about a girl called Amrita who saved her forest from a Maharaja who wanted to cut it down. She persuaded all the women in her village to stand in front of the trees. In the old story, although the forest was eventually saved, hundreds of women were killed.

The villagers of Gopeshwar were inspired by the legend and decided to protect their trees in the same way. They knew that they might be killed, like the women in the old story. Nevertheless, they decided to go ahead with their protest. Chadi Prasad Bhatt, the movement's leader, said, 'Let them know they will not fell a single tree without felling one of us first.'

They placed themselves in front of the trees. The loggers were forced to withdraw. The villagers had won and no one was killed.

A few weeks later, the loggers tried to cut down trees in the village of Rampur Phata, eighty kilometres away. The villagers of Gopeshwar heard about this and marched to Rampur Phata. They used the same tactics. Once again, they defeated the loggers.

Now the movement was big news, attracting lots of publicity. Over the next few years it grew and grew throughout northern India, and countless forests were saved.

> 'Let them know they will not fell a single tree without felling one of us first.'

In the beginning

Before reading

In groups, agree on the details of the story of Noah and the Flood. Does the story tell us anything about the way people behave? Do you know of any other myth or early story about a flood?

NOAH

They gathered around him and told him not to do it,
They formed a committee and tried to take control,
They cancelled his building permit and they stole
His pens, I sometimes wonder how he got through it.
He told them wrath was coming, they would rue it.
He begged them to believe the tides would roll,
He offered them passage to his destined goal,
A new world. They were finished and he knew it.
All to no end.
              And then the rain began.
A spatter at first that barely wet the soil,
Then showers, quick revolts lacing the town,
Then deluge universal. The old man
Arthritic from his years of scorn and toil
Leaned from the admiral's walk and watched them drown.

Roy Daniells

First impressions

What sort of person is Noah in this poem? What do you imagine his thoughts must have been as he 'watched them drown'?

Response

- Noah must have made many attempts to convince other people that the flood was coming. They obviously thought he was a nuisance and took no notice at all. In groups, write and act out a scene from early on in Noah's story, when he first hears that there will be a flood unless the people change their ways.

In the beginning

Before you begin

- Decide who is going to play which character.

- Try **improvising** the scene. Improvising means making it up as you go along without a script. Don't worry about stopping and starting again.

- When you are happy with the way it sounds, tape-record your scene. Then play it back and listen. Decide on any changes that could be made in what is said and how actors play their characters. Then try recording it again. Afterwards, you might like to write your scene up as a script.

❖ Write a story about someone who knows that a terrible disaster is coming. You might like to have an ending similar to the story of the flood, which only Noah and his family managed to survive, or you might decide to end your story quite differently.

Poetry in practice

Before you begin

- Decide when you are going to set your story. It might be now or it might be in the future.
- Decide what sort of catastrophe is going to occur.
- Decide who knows about it and why.

THE SUN WITNESS

Long ago a young girl
wearing a saffron coloured saree
walked gracefully
on her way –
She moved the square stone
from the white
near-dead grass.
By the lightning speed
of her black hand

Silently, with her gaze,
she commanded the sun
to send its light
down upon everything,
even the white grass.

The sun accepted
her easy command
and came down with humility.

Days after,
she passed beggars in the street,
and tucked in her silk saree
to avoid their stains.

Seeing this,
the sun hid behind clouds,
and rain came,
unexpectedly, like tears.

Nurunnessa Choudhurry

● In the beginning

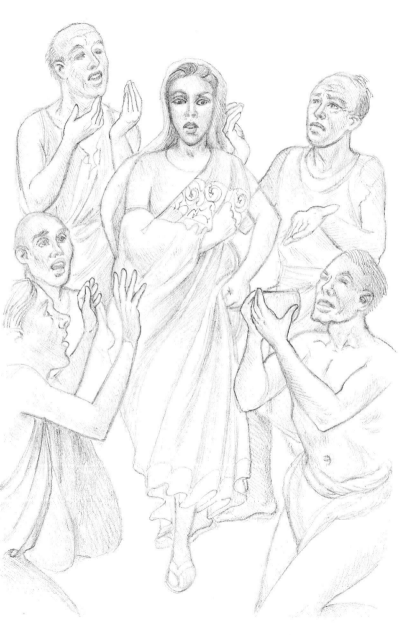

63

The shape of things to come

A CONSUMER'S REPORT

The name of the product I tested is *Life*.
I have completed the form you sent me
and understand that my answers are confidential.
I had it as a gift,
I didn't feel much while using it,
in fact I think I'd have liked to be more excited.
It seemed gentle on the hands
but left an embarrassing deposit behind.
It was not economical
and I have used much more than I thought
(I suppose I have about half left
but it's difficult to tell) –
although the instructions are fairly large
there are so many of them
I don't know which to follow, especially
as they seem to contradict each other.
I'm not sure such a thing
should be put in the way of children –
It's difficult to think of a purpose
for it. One of my friends says
it's just to keep its maker in a job.
Also the price is much too high.
Things are piling up so fast,
after all, the world got by
for a thousand million years
without this, do we need it now?
(Incidentally, please ask your man
to stop calling me 'the respondent',
I don't like the sound of it.)
There seems to be a lot of different labels,
sizes and colours should be uniform,
the shape is awkward, it's waterproof
but not heat resistant, it doesn't keep
yet it's very difficult to get rid of:
whenever they make it cheaper they seem
to put less in – if you say you don't

The shape of things to come

want it, then it's delivered anyway.
I'd agree it's a popular product,
it's got into the language; people
even say they're on the side of it.
Personally I think it's overdone,
a small thing people are ready
to behave badly about. I think
we should take it for granted. If its
experts are called philosophers or market
researchers or historians, we shouldn't
care. We are the consumers and the last
law makers. So finally, I'd buy it.
But the question of a 'best buy'
I'd like to leave until I get
the competitive product you said you'd send.

Peter Porter

Close-up

This poem is written as if it were a report on a product (like a camera or a cooker) for a consumer magazine. 'Life' is not, however, a product, so we should not take everything the poem says at face value. Many lines in this poem have more than one meaning.

In pairs, go through the poem carefully, working out what you think each line means. Then make a larger group and see if you can agree on what you think the poet is saying in the poem as a whole.

Response

❖ You could write a Consumer's Report of your own about something unusual like 'childhood' or 'happiness'.

Before you begin

Read some real consumer magazines, like *Which*, to give you ideas for the kinds of things consumers comment on.

65

'DO YOU THINK WE'LL EVER GET TO SEE EARTH, SIR?'

I hear they're hoping to run trips
one day, for the young and fit of course,
I don't see much use for it myself;
there'll be any number of places
you can't land, because they're still toxic,
and even in the relatively safe bits
you won't see what it was; what it could be.
I can't fancy a tour through the ruins
Of my home with a party of twenty-five
and a guide to tell me what to see.
But if you should see some beautiful thing,
some leaf, say, damascined with frost,
some iridescence on a pigeon's neck,
some stone, some curve, some clear water;
look at it as if you were made of eyes,
as if you were nothing but an eye, lidless
and tender to be probed and scorched
by extreme light. Look at it with your skin,
with the small hairs on the back of your neck.
If it is well-shaped, look at it with your hands;
If it has fragrance, breathe it into yourself;
if it tastes sweet, put your tongue to it.
Look at it as a happening, a moment;
Let nothing of it go unrecorded,
map it as if it were already passing.
Look at it for later, look at it for ever,
and look at it once for me.

Sheenagh Pugh

The shape of things to come

Poetry in practice

Before reading

Write down all the words that you associate with the two words 'revolution' and 'evolution'. Look them up in a dictionary and make a note of some of the meanings you discover.

Try not to be put off by the fact that this is quite a long poem. Since winning the London Weekend Television/ILEA Poetry Competition in 1989, it has been read by many people of your age.

You might like to read it out loud in groups.

EVOLUTION REVOLUTION

PHASE ONE. COMPLEX BUT CRUCIAL

It seemed so trivial.
He locked the doors,
Checked the boot, and left.
He didn't hear the piercing alarm
Which some careless commuter set off
By hitting the wing with his briefcase.
But it cried, so shrill and persistent
In a haze of ecstatic release
To be at last fulfilling its function –
Namely to wail aloud, to get attention.
It felt worthwhile at last,
And like the Sirens, like the drone of the doodlebug,
Like the horn of the car you stepped out in front of,
Like the four-minute warning,
It spelled danger.

The car next to it also had an alarm.
Whether through freak conditions,
Sound or electric waves,
Or the all-penetrating force of ecstasy,
The alarm next door realised what was going on.
It sensed the freedom, the joy, the exhilaration,
And it too decided that,
Since its sole reason for existence was to wail,
Then wail it would.
And did.
And the fever began to spread.

The shape of things to come

Seventy-seven car alarms started, one by one.
Then house alarms, then shop alarms;
All across the
Town
District
County
Region
Country, cars and houses, shops and depots,
Museums and palaces and police stations screamed.
The people raged and wondered.
But the machines, invented then neglected,
Began to feel the change:
The catalyst came cataclysmically.

The vintage motorcycle had sat beneath the sheet
For years. Had it been invented to sit beneath a sheet?
No, it had not. It existed to speed,
To travel, to conquer.
And as the car that shared its garage shrieked
And the house adjoined to it sirened
The motorcycle got the message

And roared
And moved
And rode, riderless, fulfilled,
Screaming past screaming homes and screaming homeowners.

Poetry in practice

And of course the first fatality was a
Shock.
How many riderless vehicles knock down pedestrians?
Up till then – not many.
After then –
Many.

So – alarms wailed, vehicles sped,
Lawnmowers mowed,
Record players played,
Chainsaws sawed,
Electric toothbrushes brushed electrically.
Rifles fired, antique cannons boomed,
Tourist attraction battleships upped anchor
And made battle; and bridges whose middle sections lifted,
Lifted to let them through.

Things made to move, moved.
Things made to flash, flashed.
Things made to emit noise, emitted.
Things made to kill insects, killed.
Things made to kill rodents, killed.
Things made to kill fish, killed.
Things made to kill men,
Killed.

And after the first phase of the revolution was in full swing,
The most amazing thing was not the sight, the smell,
The danger or the death-roll,
But the noise.
It was really very noisy indeed.

PHASE TWO. SIMPLE AND PRETTY.

The shed pondered politics beneath its roofing felt.
It seemed unfair that
The lawnmower, hedgetrimmer, bicycles and drill
Which the shed had used to hold
Could fulfil their creations,
While the shed itself
Could do nothing at all.
A shed, it thought, is a shed, is a shed.
Or . . . ?

And then a ticklish sort of thought occurred to it.
An inkling perhaps, or an intuition,
That maybe its fundamental function was NOT
To house horticulture,
But instead maybe it was to grow leaves,
Nestle birds,
Take in water through roots,
And be coated in bark,
Not creosote.

OK then, thought the shed, I'll give it a go.
And it did.

There, that's much better, thought the
Tree.
Much more comfy.
Pleasant. Natural.

Poetry in practice

Cardboard, pencils, matches,
Shakespeare's pages, the Turin Shroud,
And Lady Di's wedding dress,
All decided that plants were much nicer things to be than
Boxes, pencils, matches,
Plays, sheets or dresses,
So they did something about it.

And suddenly there were a lot more plants and trees.
A lot less factories and houses
And tarmac and sheds and clothes.
Oh, and pencils too.

PHASE THREE. IT GETS QUIETER AGAIN.

A motorcycle with sidecar drove into an oak tree
And smashed.
And all its mangled pieces felt
Unusually unfulfilled,
And decided that,
Rather than being a buckled bike,
It would be nice to be
Elements and ores, deep beneath the soil,
Simply existing as minerals,
And smiling a bit too.

First of all individual nuts and bolts,
Then spokes, gear cables,
Frame, dials, exhaust pipe, engine,
All shifted, parted and coagulated,
Unsmelted themselves,
And in their various primitive forms,
Burrowed, wriggled and soaked into the ground;
And felt good.

And the plastics mingled with the
Newly unrefined fuels, rebecame oils, and seeped in harmony,
Back to where they all belonged.

All the hectic, chaotic, manic machines
Began to think hard,
And they too considered whether
Shaving beards off, ironing things flat or
Shooting things dead
Were more satisfying than passive, prehistoric

The shape of things to come

Pre-interfered with existence
Beneath the earth –
At home.

Knives and forks,
Concorde,
Nail clippers,
The Eiffel Tower,
Digital alarm clocks and
The Statue of Liberty
All went,
And felt much better.

Funnily enough, that first car alarm
Was one of the last to go. It had been
Wallowing in its wailing so much
That the message had taken some time to get through.
But that's not important now.
It's all past history now.

Poetry in practice

PHASE FOUR. PROBABLY THE BEST BIT.

It was now rather quiet again.
But that didn't last.
Basically, there were
A lot more jungles and forests and meadows,
And a lot less cages and zoos and labs.
So what do you expect?
The animals moved home.

And so, of course,
What with calls, and cries, and crows,
Roars, songs, whistles and woofs,
It was rather noisy again.
But a different sort of noise
Which seemed to fit quite well.
So nobody minded this time.

PHASE FIVE. SHORT AND UNIMPORTANT.

It took a long time to get through to the men.
But at last it happened.
A man, recently denuded and stripped of his quartz analogue,
Saw a Volvo bearing down on him.
So he climbed up a tree.
Looking down, he saw the Volvo wasn't there any more,
And was just about to climb out of his tree,
When he realised he quite liked it,
And stayed there.

Andrew Smith (aged 17)

● The shape of things to come

ANDREW SMITH

We ignore the facts about the environment and the natural world which are so important.

How old were you when you wrote 'Evolution Revolution?'
Seventeen.

Where do you get your inspiration?
I just wait for it to happen. Like this one begins with a car burglar alarm and it was hearing one of those going off every morning that started me thinking about the poem.

How do you actually go about writing a poem?
Well, generally it all comes out at once first time, and then I often have to leave it a while and look over it again and again to get the details right, get it sounding exactly right.

Details seem to be very important to you. In 'Evolution Revolution' you pick on particular details – electric toothbrushes or the Turin Shroud. Is this the way you normally write?
I think so. I use close-ups on small things to speak about the overall effect.

What were you trying to say when you wrote this poem?
That we rely too much on technology. We ignore the facts about the environment and the natural world which are so important.

What is happening in the poem?
The first stage shows technology going wild, much further than it has actually gone. It's meant to be almost like science fiction. Then the natural world says it's had enough of this and takes over and sets evolution into reverse. I don't suppose, actually, that this is something that is ever going to happen, although it might be the best thing for the world!

Did you deliberately try to see this from the point of view of some of the objects in the poem?
Yes. I found myself thinking that I would get very frustrated if I were a burglar alarm. I'd want to hang on the wall and make a lot of noise and not wait for someone to break into the building. After all, that is what I was built for.

Who did you have in mind as an audience when you wrote this poem?
I think I was just writing it for myself, but I hope that people of all ages might find it interesting.

Poetry in practice

First impressions

In your group, take it in turns to describe anything at all that occurred to you as you read this poem. Make a list of your group's first reactions.

Close-up

- It sometimes helps to know what was in the poet's mind when he or she was writing a particular poem. Here and on pages 30–1 there are Back-Up Files, containing interviews with young poets who describe what they were thinking about at the time of writing.

  Do you agree with Andrew Smith's view that we rely too much on technology? Can you think of examples which support your views?

- When you are reading a long poem like this one, if often helps to break it up into smaller sections while you are trying to understand what the poet is saying.

  In groups, using the five sections into which 'Evolution Revolution' has been divided, make a cartoon strip version of the poem. If you draw this to a large scale, you could produce it as a poster for your wall. You could also rewrite the poem underneath as a simple commentary, to reinforce the message.

- In groups, choose one line from each part of the poem that you think best sums up the meaning of that particular section. Compare your group's choices with others in the class. Now compare the lines you have chosen with the titles Andrew Smith gives for each section. Which do you prefer? Give your reasons. As a class, try to decide on a new, shortened version of the poem, using only one line from each section.

Response

In his interview, Andrew Smith explains how he enjoys using 'close-ups' in his poems. He says that he likes to pick on important details. So, to make his point about technology, he goes into 'close-up' on burglar alarms, chain-saws, lawn mowers, etc.

Andrew Smith's poem uses **fantasy**. Writing a fantasy poem or story means making up a world which does not or could not exist. 'Evolution Revolution' is a fantasy because machines like lawn mowers could not possibly come to life.

- Write your own fantasy poem about the future. It could be about a bizarre revolution like the one in the poem you have just read. Try to concentrate on events (what is happening) rather than on descriptions of what your idea of the future is like.

Before you begin

- Decide what it is that will make your story fantastic.

- Decide what sort of details you want to concentrate on.

- Decide whether you want to divide your poem up into stages as Andrew Smith has done.

The heart of the matter

Poems in Pairs

THE MOTH

The moth is a fat, stubby glider;
Its wedge-shaped wings of blotchy rose-petal
Flutter madly,
Almost too madly to be graceful.
But it is,
As it flits and hovers,
Like a dandelion clock caught in an unsteady breeze.

Its body is a cream eclair,
Ready to split at the slightest squeeze.
Its eyes are tiny
Pinheads on a tight bundle of rags,
Pushed down in the toe of an old stocking.
And its legs aren't legs;
They are runners – Not for walking,
But hanging and standing.

The moth is a crippled angel.
It worships light,
As if it were a god; it stays with it,
Rarely leaving.
But the moth is an insect,
A soldier of fortune.
And a new battle for survival
Dawns every day.

Stephen Gardam (aged 12)

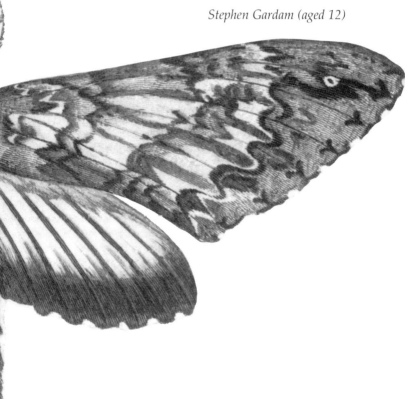

Poetry in practice

THE SPIDER

The spider, a mistake
On God's paper.
A thumb print of ink
That splattered eight ways.
He hides guiltily in shadows,
And scurries, face lowered.
He's accused of a crime
That he didn't commit.
The crime is life,
So he hides away from it,
And takes revenge
On content thieves
That stole freedom.
But he is a spider,
A mistake on God's paper.
A mistake never to be forgiven.

Thea Smiley (aged 13)

Close-up

Both these poems work by being original. The poets describe their subjects in unusual ways and because of this the descriptions are very effective.

Stephen Gardam, for example, describes the moth as if it were a glider. We realise that this cannot be so, but understand what he is trying to say. Describing one thing as if it were something quite different is known as using a **metaphor**. The technique is similar to using a simile, although the words of comparison – 'as' or 'like' – are not included. In this particular instance, describing a moth as if it were a glider means that all the characteristics of the aircraft are transferred to the insect, so making the description more vivid and therefore more effective.

Look at the kinds of metaphors Stephen Gardam and Thea Smiley use in their poems. These work in different ways. Sometimes they seem right because of the pictures they conjure up, sometimes it is one of our senses that is being appealed to, and sometimes it is the idea behind the picture that makes the comparison effective.

Pick two or three of the metaphors and decide what it is that gives them their force.

Response

- Write your own group poem about an animal or an insect.

Before you begin

- Agree on the subject of your poem.

- Working together, brainstorm as many different ideas about your subject as possible. Think of things that your animal or insect reminds you of. Try to think of unusual ways of describing it.

- Pick out those ideas which really get to the heart of your subject.

Poetry in practice

RIDDLE

I am the shame beneath a carpet.
No one comes to sweep me off my feet.

Abandoned rooms and unread books collect me.
Sometimes I dance like particles of light.

My legions thicken on each window pane,
A gathering of dusk, perpetual gloom.

And when at last the house has fallen,
I am the cloud left hanging in the air.

(Ans: dust)

John Mole

Response

Riddles are very often written in the **first person**. That means using the word 'I' (for example, 'I am the shame beneath a carpet').

❖ Try making up your own riddles, writing them in the first person. When you have finished, you could put them all together in a class collection.

Before you begin

- Decide on your subject.
- Decide on its strongest characteristics.
- Decide how to describe your subject in a way that disguises it.

ONE QUESTION FROM A BULLET

I want to give up being a bullet
I've been a bullet too long

I want to be an innocent coin
in the hand of a child
and be squeezed through the slot
of a bubblegum machine

I want to give up being a bullet
I've been a bullet too long

I want to be a good luck seed
lying idle in somebody's pocket
or some ordinary little stone
on the way to becoming an earring
or just lying there unknown
among a crowd of other ordinary stones.

I want to give up being a bullet
I've been a bullet too long

The question is
Can you give up being a killer?

John Agard

RAW CARROTS

Raw carrots taste
Cool and hard,
Like some crisp metal.

Horses are
Fond of them,
Crunching up

The red gold
With much wet
Juice and noise.

Carrots must taste
To horses
As they do to us.

Valerie Worth

Things are not what they seem

THE SEA

The sea is a hungry dog,
Giant and grey.
He rolls on the beach all day.
With his clashing teeth and shaggy jaws
Hour upon hour he gnaws
The rumbling, tumbling stones,
And 'Bones, bones, bones, bones!'
The giant sea-dog moans,
Licking his greasy paws.

And when the night wind roars
And the moon rocks in the stormy cloud,
He bounds to his feet and snuffs and sniffs,
Shaking his wet sides over the cliffs,
And howls and hollos long and loud.

But on quiet days in May or June,
When even the grasses on the dune
Play no more their reedy tune,
With his head between his paws
He lies on the sandy shores,
So quiet, so quiet, he scarcely snores.

James Reeves

Close-up

Writers often talk of the importance of trying to bring their subject to life. One way of doing this is to compare the subject to something else, using similes and metaphors (see pages 37 and 82). This technique can be used to build up the atmosphere of a poem.

James Reeves could have compared the sea to quite a different animal, but he chose a dog. Different creatures mean different things to us. In groups, look at this list and decide what qualities you associate with each creature:

eagle, shark, lion, mouse, horse, butterfly, cat, snake, scorpion.

What sort of moods might these creatures have?

Why do you think James Reeves chose to compare the sea to a dog?

Response

❖ Create your own soundtrack for 'The Sea'.

Before you begin

• Think about the sort of sounds that the sea makes.

• Reread the poem and make up your mind what the poet thinks about the sea.

• Pick out words in the poem that suggest sounds to you.

• Choose music that you think best suits the mood of this poem and make a tape-recording of it.

• Play the music as you read the poem to the rest of your class.

Poetry in practice

Poems in Paris

Before reading

Make a list of the words that you associate with:

- November;
- fog.

THE FOG

I saw the fog grow thick,
   Which soon made blind my ken;
It made tall men of boys,
   And giants of tall men.

It clutched my throat, I coughed;
   Nothing was in my head
Except two heavy eyes
   Like balls of burning lead.

And when it grew so black
   That I could know no place,
I lost all judgement then,
   Of distance and of space.

The street lamps, and the lights
   Upon the halted cars,
Could either be on earth
   Or be the heavenly stars.

A man passed me by close,
   I asked my way, he said,
'Come, follow me, my friend –'
   I followed where he led.

He rapped the stones in front,
   'Trust me,' he said, 'and come';
I followed like a child –
   A blind man led me home.

W. H. Davies

NOVEMBER STORY

The evening had caught cold;
Its eyes were blurred.
It had a dripping nose
And its tongue was furred.

I sat in a warm bar
After a day's work;
November snuffled outside,
Greasing the sidewalk.

But soon I had to go
Out into the night
Where shadows prowled the alleys,
Hiding from the light.

But light shone at the corner
On the pavement where
A man had fallen over
Or been knocked down there.

His legs on the slimed concrete
Were splayed out wide;
He had been propped against a lamp-post;
His head lolled to one side.

A victim of crime or accident,
An image of fear,
He remained quite motionless
As I drew near.

Then a thin voice startled silence
From a doorway close by
Where an urchin hid from the wind:
'Spare a penny for the guy!'

I gave the boy some money
And hastened on.
A voice called, 'Thank you guv'nor!'
And the words upon

The wincing air seemed strange –
So hoarse and deep –
As if the guy had spoken
In his restless sleep.

Vernon Scannell

Poetry in practice

Close-up

Describe the atmosphere created at the beginning of each of these poems. Select the lines that do most to produce this atmosphere. Explain your choices.

How does the atmosphere change at the end of each poem?

Response

- Make up your own poem about someone going for a walk. It should start with a strong sense of atmosphere and have a surprise ending.

Before you begin

- Think carefully about the atmosphere you want to produce. Use metaphors to help create it. (See p. 83 for an explanation of metaphors.)

- Decide how your poem will end.

Relationships

Poems in Pairs

NOBODY'S FAULT

Husband It's your father's fault.
When he arranged our marriage
He never told me
You talked so much!
That day I went to visit –
Four cups of tea
I drank
And sat there for an hour.
Not a word!
I practically begged you to speak to me.

Wife Well what do you expect?
Our four parents watching
With eager smiles
And I was pouring the tea
And my dupatta kept slipping off.
It's not easy you know!

Husband And those spectacles –
You didn't wear them that day.
And now I must spend a fortune
On contact lenses.

Wife You're right of course.
If I'd worn them
I'd never have married
Such an ugly man.

Husband And cooking –
'She loves cooking,' your mother told me.
After a hard day I come home
And what do we have?
Take-aways!

Wife Well, you never like the things I cook.
My byriani
Went in the bin, you know,

Husband And who pays for them?
Me, of course.
To pay for take-away food
I work the whole day.

Poetry in practice

Wife   I worked all day to cook byriani,
Phoned up mum,
Asked for the recipe three times.

Husband And the phone bill gets bigger.
I pay for the phone bill,
For burnt food,
For take-aways,
And for what?
Why did I marry?
Only to please my father.

Wife   Your father?
What about me?
I never dreamt that things would be like this
That day my father said to you,
'Look after her, she's my favourite
And I have brought her up
Like a princess,'
And you shook his hand
And said,
'Yes'.

Husband Now look, don't cry.
Come on,
Stop that now.
You know I never mean
The things I say.
Please cheer up.
All right,
All right, I agree.
I'll go and get a take-away!

Shahana Mirza

Close-up

Read the poem again. Try to decide whether:

- the characters have had this conversation, or one like it, before;

- this is a major quarrel or just a small argument;

- they are talking to each other or shouting.

Now read the poem out loud in pairs, one of you taking the part of the husband, the other the part of the wife. Try to sound as if you really mean what you are saying!

LONG DISTANCE PHONE CALL: MICHAEL TO GERALDINE

GERALDINE SPEAKING:

Hallo, lovely of you to ring.

NAOMI SIT DOWN

Where are you now?
Oh nice. Have you got a telly in your room?

NO, YOU'RE NOT WATCHING TELLY NOW. IT'S BED TIME

No, not you, you fool, you can go to bed anytime you like.
It's been absolutely terrible here. I'm shattered.

PUT IT DOWN LAURA. PUT IT DOWN. NAOMI HELP HER

Would you believe it? She can see I'm on the phone and she
    can't even help Laura with her corn flakes . . .

AND NOW IT'S ALL OVER THE FLOOR. YOU FOOL.

Of course it's not your fault, Michael.
So. Have you been busy?

NAOMI, COULDN'T YOU SEE IT?

She stood in it. Right in it.

THEY'RE ALL OVER YOUR SHOE, GIRL.
DON'T BE SO CLUMSY.
CAN'T YOU SEE I'M ON THE PHONE. JUST PLAY
    WITH HER
KEEP HER HAPPY

You sound ever so far away.
Yes, I suppose Singapore is a long way away now I
    think of it.

TAKE HER AWAY FROM IT.
I DON'T WANT HER TO PRETEND TO DO THE WASHING UP
    IN IT.
NAOMI, CAN YOU HEAR ME?
I DON'T WANT HER TO WASH UP WITH THE CORNFLAKES

The builders have made a terrible mess with the wall.

NOT ON ME, LAURA.

Poetry in practice

You know what she's done? Yes. All down my skirt.
I can't describe it.
Oh, you mean the wall.
No I can't describe that either.

NAOMI, QUICK TAKE HER THERE IF SHE WANTS TO GO.
NO, MUMMY CAN'T TAKE YOU, LAURA. I'M ON THE PHONE.
GO ON TAKE HER THERE, NAOMI. YOU'VE DONE IT BEFORE,
    HAVEN'T YOU?
JUST SIT HER ON IT AND STAY WITH HER

Would you believe it, she won't go unless I take her.
Look, it's lovely of you to ring.

STOP SCREAMING. I CAN'T HEAR A WORD MICHAEL'S SAYING

What do you mean the hotel collapsed?
Oh no, she's done it.

NAOMI, YOU COULD HAVE TRIED.
LAURA, YOU KNOW THAT'S NAUGHTY
YOU KNOW NOT TO DO IT ON THE FLOOR

Did you say collapsed?

A CLOTH. A CLOTH. ANY CLOTH. A KITCHEN
    TOWEL. A PAPER HANKIE.
ANYTHING, NAOMI.

She behaves like she's never spilt anything in her life, my
mother would have tanned the backside off me if I behaved like
her, you know.
Not *your* hotel?

I'LL TELL YOU WHAT HE SAYS IN A MINUTE.
YOU DO WHAT YOU'VE GOT TO DO
AND LEAVE ME TO TALK TO MICHAEL
WAIT LAURA

Can you hear? Isn't that sweet?
Laura wants to say hallo.

LET LAURA SAY HELLO FIRST, NAOMI

She's tried to snatch it off Laura.

REALLY, NAOMI. THINGS LIKE THAT MAKE HER SCREAM.
NOW SAY HALLO TO DADDO, LAURA.

● Relationships

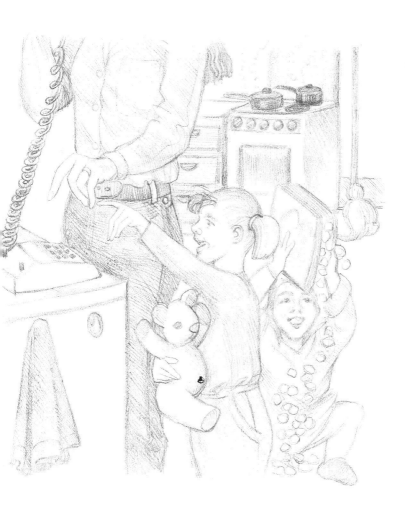

MIND THE CORNFLAKES . . . TOO LATE. NEVER MIND

She says she doesn't want to say hallo to fatbum.
Look, are you all right?
What is it, an earthquake or something?
Hallo?
Hallo?
Hallo?

Hallo?

Michael Rosen

Poetry in practice

Response

❖ In 'Long Distance Phone Call: Michael to Geraldine' you get only one side of a conversation. You don't hear what Michael says. Working on your own, reread the poem carefully and decide what he might be saying in reply to each of Geraldine's statements. Has the hotel really collapsed? Arrange Michael's replies into a poem which you might like to call 'Long Distance Phone Call: Geraldine to Michael'.

❖ Both 'Nobody's Fault' and 'Long Distance Phone Call: Michael to Geraldine' are poems about people's family lives. They deal with the way that people who live together treat one another. Both poems are written as conversations. Write your own conversation poem between two people who spend their lives together. Remember, they don't have to be husband and wife.

Before you begin

• Decide how many characters you are going to have and which ones will speak. It will help to look back to the poems you have just read.

• Decide what the characters are going to talk about. Will they have a quarrel, as in 'Nobody's Fault'? Will they be interrupted all the time as in Michael Rosen's poem, or will they succeed in having a proper conversation?

• Decide how your conversation is going to end. Will it be cut off abruptly? Will it come to a definite conclusion?

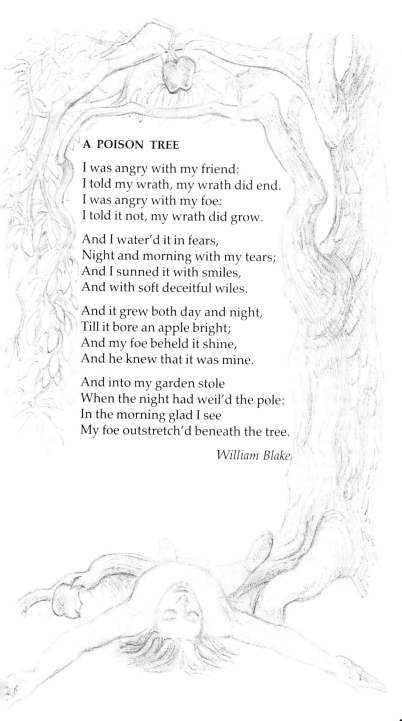

A POISON TREE

I was angry with my friend:
I told my wrath, my wrath did end.
I was angry with my foe:
I told it not, my wrath did grow.

And I water'd it in fears,
Night and morning with my tears;
And I sunned it with smiles,
And with soft deceitful wiles.

And it grew both day and night,
Till it bore an apple bright;
And my foe beheld it shine,
And he knew that it was mine.

And into my garden stole
When the night had weil'd the pole:
In the morning glad I see
My foe outstretch'd beneath the tree.

William Blake

Poetry in practice

First impressions

Which of the following statements seem to relate in some way to what William Blake is saying in this poem? In groups, discuss each one in turn, commenting on its connection with 'A Poison Tree'.

- Blake was a gardener.
- Blake was angry.
- There are different ways of dealing with anger.
- It is dangerous for anyone to bottle up their anger.
- It is dangerous for other people if you bottle up your anger.
- Anger is a good thing.
- Anger is like an apple.
- Anger can leave a nasty taste in your mouth.
- Anger can kill.

Close-up

In this poem, William Blake describes a certain kind of anger growing in the ground like an apple pip. Instead of producing a delicious fruit, it produces a poisonous one. As we have already seen (p. 83) this technique is called using a **metaphor**. We know that anger cannot really be planted in the ground, but we understand what Blake is trying to tell us.

Blake does not leave the fruit metaphor there, however. He continues it through the poem, so turning 'A Poison Tree' into an **allegory**, or extended metaphor. In an allegory, the writer tells a story using symbolic objects or events in order to explain an idea. In this case, for example, the pip, the apple tree and the garden are all symbols used by Blake to put across his views on anger.

In groups, decide what it is that Blake is trying to tell us about anger through his use of allegory in this poem.

Some people find the ending of the poem unclear. They are not sure why Blake's enemy dies. What do you think about this?

Response

'A Poison Tree' was written two hundred years ago and first appeared in Blake's collection of poems called *Songs of Innocence and Experience*. Blake felt it was important to use images or pictures to put across his ideas, so he illustrated each poem himself. The picture shown here is based on his illustration for 'A Poison Tree'.

- In his painting, William Blake tried to sum up the whole poem. Another way of doing this would be to produce a cartoon version of the poem. Design your own set of cartoon illustrations for 'A Poison Tree' for a class display.

Before you begin

- Reread the poem. Follow Blake's allegory of how he 'grew' his anger.

- Decide what is happening in each part of the description and what your illustration will show. It might help to plan your cartoon strip as a storyboard, which is a rough set of sketches, giving an idea of what will appear in the finished version.

Blue for a girl

THREE POEMS FOR WOMEN

1

This is a poem for a woman doing dishes.
This is a poem for a woman doing dishes.
It must be repeated.
It must be repeated,
again and again,
again and again,
because the woman doing dishes
because the woman doing dishes
has trouble hearing
has trouble hearing.

2

And this is another poem for a woman
cleaning the floor
who cannot hear at all.
Let us have a moment of silence
for the woman who cleans the floor.

3

And here is one more poem
for the woman at home
with children.
You never see her at night.
Stare at an empty space and imagine her there,
the woman with children
because she cannot be here to speak
for herself,
and listen
to what you think
she might say.

Susan Griffin

First impressions

Read 'Three Poems for Women' again. In pairs, jot down your first reactions to the poem and then exchange them with your partner. Comment on what your partner has written.

Close-up

Susan Griffin describes women involved in three activities in the home.

• Which activities or occupations are often associated with women?

• Which activities or occupations do women rarely do?

• Are there any activities or occupations you can't imagine women doing often? At all?

Response

❖ Write your own version of 'Three Poems for Women' in which you select three activities of your choice.

Before you begin

• Read this well-known riddle:

A man and his son are involved in a fatal car crash. The man is killed and the son seriously injured. The boy is rushed to hospital in an ambulance and taken straight to the operating theatre. The surgeon comes in, takes one look at the boy and says, 'I can't operate. That's my son.' How can this be?

What do you think the answer is, and what does it tell you about your own attitudes?

• Look at the way in which Susan Griffin has written her first poem. She repeats lines to make a point about the woman's life. You might like to try using a similar technique.

A WOMAN'S PLACE

At home

(from the *Guardian*, 26 March, 1991)

Lack of child care facilities prevents women, as opposed to men, from pursuing their careers.

Percentage of parents with children aged 0–4 who work

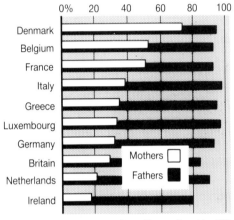

Source: European Commision, 1985

At work

During the past 20 years earnings have improved, but women are still paid about a quarter less than men for doing similar work.

Average gross hourly earnings (pence per hour)

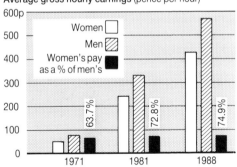

Source: New Earnings Survey

Poetry in practice

Poems in Pairs

Before reading

In groups, remind yourselves of the stories of Cinderella and Snow White and the Seven Dwarfs.

INTERVIEW

Yes, this is where she lived before she won
The title Miss Glass Slipper of the Year,
And went to the ball and married the king's son.
You're from the local press, and want to hear
About her early life? Young man, sit down.
These are my two own daughters; you'll not find
Nicer, more biddable girls in all the town,
And lucky, I tell them, not to be the kind

That Cinderella was, spreading those lies,
Telling those shameless tales about the way
We treated her. Oh, nobody denies
That she was pretty if you like those curls.
But looks aren't everything, I always say.
Be sweet and natural, I tell my girls,
And Mr Right will come along, some day.

Sara Henderson Hay

ONE OF THE SEVEN HAS SOMETHING TO SAY

Remember how it was before she came – ?
The picks and shovels dropped beside the door,
The sink piled high, the meals any old time,
Our jackets where we'd flung them on the floor?
The mud tracked in, the clutter on the shelves.
None of us shaved, or more than halfway clean . . .
Just seven old bachelors, living by ourselves?
Those were the days, if you know what I mean.

She scrubs, she sweeps, she even dusts the ceilings;
She's made us build a tool shed for our stuff.
Dinner's at eight, the table setting's formal
And if I weren't afraid I'd hurt her feelings
I'd move, until we get her married off,
And things can gradually slip back to normal.

Sara Henderson Hay

First impressions

Look at the following statements about the two poems. Which ones are closest to your own opinions? Add some statements of your own which say what you think the poems are about.

- Fairy stories have nothing to do with real life.

- Most fairy stories are sexist.

- Little children should not be told fairy stories.

- Fairy stories are harmless.

- Everyone needs fairy stories.

- These two poems have nothing to do with fairy stories.

- Just because Cinderella was beautiful, it doesn't mean she was nice.

- Snow White needed the Dwarfs more than they needed her.

Response

 Reread 'Interview'. Notice how the story is told as if the stepmother were being interviewed by a reporter. In pairs, act out the interview.

Before you begin

• Decide which one of you is going to be the reporter and which one the stepmother.

• Decide what questions the reporter will ask.

• If you are the reporter, add some extra questions of your own during the interview to make it more natural.

• Decide how the interview will end. You might like to add your own surprise fairy-tale ending.

• Tape-record your interview and listen to how it sounds. Make any changes you feel are appropriate and then record it again. Afterwards, you might like to write up your interview as a script.

HER GREATEST LOVE

At sixty she's experiencing
the greatest love of her life.

She walks arm in arm with her lover,
the wind ruffles their grey hair.

Her lover says:
– 'You have hair like pearls.'

Her children say:
– 'You silly old fool.'

Anna 'Swir'

SHE REALISED

On Sunday afternoon
with the washing-up finally done,
she sat down
in front of the mirror.

And she realised
on Sunday afternoon
that she'd been robbed of her life.

A long time ago.

Anna 'Swir'

Beans, greens and tangerines

HEALTH FANATIC

around the block against the clock
tick tock tick tock tick tick tock
running out of breath running out of socks
rubber on the road flippety flop
non-skid agility chop chop
no time to hang about
work out health fanatic work out

the crack of dawn lifting weights
a tell-tale heart reverberates
high in polyunsaturates
low in polysaturates
a duke of edinburgh's award awaits
it's a man's life
he's a health fanatic so was his wife

a one-man war against decay
enjoys himself the hard way
allows himself a mars a day
how old am i what do i weigh
punch me there does it hurt no way
running on the spot don't get too hot
he's a health fanatic that's why not

running through the traffic jam taking in the lead
hyperactivity keeps him out of bed
deep down he'd like to kick it in the head
they'll regret it when they're dead
there's more to life than fun
he's a health fanatic he's got to run

beans greens and tangerines
and low cholesterol margarines
his limbs are loose his teeth are clean
he's a high octane fresh-air fiend
you've got to admit he's keen
what can you do but be impressed?
he's a health fanatic give it a rest

Beans, greens and tangerines

shadow boxing punch the wall
one-a-side football
what's the score one all
could have been a copper too small
could have been a jockey too tall
knees up knees up head the ball
nervous energy makes him tick
he's a health fanatic he makes you sick

John Cooper Clarke

Poetry in practice

ABOUT AUNTIE ROSE & HER DIET

my auntie rose says
'no sugar for me
just a little artificial sweetener
in my cup of tea'

she says
'just half a slice
of that lovely cake.
it looks so nice'

so she eats one half slice
& another half slice
& another half slice
& another
& another
& another

& her eyes glaze
i can almost see her
growing fatter & fatter
till the cake's all gone & then
she says 'oh well
it doesn't matter
there's another one in the fridge
on a baked meringue platter.'

when she's eaten that she laughs
she says 'my clothes don't fit me
any more' & we're off on the bus
to the larger ladies' fashion store

after that she says, 'my word,
that's really worn me out
it must be lunchtime
my stomach's crying out for food.'

in the coffee shop she says,
i'm back on the diet
no sugar for me
just a little artificial sweetener
in my cup of tea
that dress i bought
is on the big side, so while we're here
let's have a pie
& half a slice of that lovely cake
it looks so nice . . .'

Jenny Boult

Poetry in practice

Before reading

In groups, agree on the details of the Frankenstein story. There is more than one version, so try to decide on the original storyline.

BURGER BEAST

The giant thing,
With the hamburger head,
Ate everything in its sight,
But for its favourite food,
It had to bend,
Way down,
To the ground,
To catch small children.
'Scrunch, Scrunch',
How it loved to crunch them.

It was a nightmarish day.
As it came to life,
People finally realised
They were not eating food,
At all,
The food was eating them.

The hamburger thing,
Created by men,
Was fooled by women.
They shouted up at it,
It slowly nodded its head.

This was the deal.
'Since Frankensteins, in the end,
Always turn on their makers,'
They said,
'Save yourself some trouble,
Why not eat the men, instead.'

Everyone agreed how peaceful it was,
Once the last man,
Disappeared down the thing's bun.

Maria Maryon

Close-up

- Why does Maria Maryon blame men for creating the Burger Beast? Doing some research on the hamburger industry might help you to answer this. Try to find out:

    - how big the hamburger industry is;
    - who it is run by;
    - what effect producing hamburgers has on the environment;
    - what effect consuming them has.

- What do you think Maria Maryon is saying by making women defeat the Burger Beast? Do you agree with her?

Shopping

Poems in Pairs

GRANNY IN DE MARKET PLACE

Yuh fish fresh?

Woman, why yuh holdin' meh fish up tuh yuh nose?
De fish fresh. Ah say it fresh. Ah ehn go say it any mo'

Hmmm, well if dis fish fresh den is I who dead an' gone
De ting smell like it take a bath in a lavatory in town
It here so long it happy. Look how de mout' laughin' at we
De eye turn up to heaven like it want tuh know 'e fate
Dey say it does take a good week before dey reach dat state

Yuh mango ripe?

Gran'ma, stop feelin' and squeezin' up meh fruit!
Yuh ehn playin' in no ban'. Meh mango eh no concertina

Ah tell yuh dis mango hard just like yuh face
One bite an' ah sure tuh break both ah meh plate
If yuh cahn tell de difference between green an' rosy red
dohn clim' jus' wait until dey fall down from de tree
Yuh go know dey ripe when de lizard an dem start tuh feed
but dohn bring yuh force-ripe fruit tuh try an' sell in here
it ehn burglars is crooks like all yuh poor people have to fear

De yam good?

Old lady; get yuh nails outta meh yam!
Ah mad tuh make yuh buy it now yuh damage it so bad

Dis yam look like de one dat did come off ah de ark
She brother in de Botanical Gardens up dey by Queens Park
Tourists with dey camera comin' from all over de worl'
takin' pictures dey never hear any yam could be dat ole
Ah have a crutch an' a rocking-chair someone give meh fur free
If ah did know ah would ah bring dem an' leave dem here fuh
  she

De bush clean?

Well, I never hear more! Old woman, is watch yuh watching meh
young young dasheen leaf wit' de dew still shinin' on dem!

It seem tuh me like dey does like tuh lie out in de sun
jus' tuh make sure dat dey get dey edges nice an' brown
an' maybe is weight dey liftin' tuh make dem look so tough
Dey wan' build up dey strength fuh when tings start gettin' rough
Is callaloo ah makin' but ah 'fraid tings go get too hot
Yuh bush go want tuh fight an' meh crab go jump outta de pot

How much a poun' yuh fig?

Ah have a big big sign tellin' yuh how much it cos'
Yuh either blin' yuh dotish or yuh jus' cahn read at all

Well, ah wearing meh glasses so ah readin' yuh big big sign
but tuh tell yuh de trut' ah jus' cahn believe meh eye
Ah lookin' ah seein' but no man could be so blasted bol'
Yuh mus' tink dis is Fort Knox yuh sellin' fig as if is gol'
Dey should put all ah all yuh somewhere nice an' safe
If dey ehn close Sing-Sing prison dat go be the bestest place

De orange sweet?

Ma, it eh hah orange in dis market as sweet as ah does sell
It like de sun, it taste like sugar an' it juicy as well

Yuh know, boy, what you sayin' have a sorta ring
De las' time ah buy yuh tell meh exactly de same ting
When ah suck ah fin' all ah dem sour as hell
De dentures drop out an' meh two gum start tuh swell
Meh mout' so sore ah cahn even eat ah meal
Yuh sure it ehn lime all you wrappin' in orange peel?

De coconut hah water?

Amryl Johnson

Poetry in practice

SHOPPING

look over there in that window
isn't that lovely
the sort of thing that would
go with your hair
it would look nice on you

we'll go & try it on
shall we?
well, all right. perhaps not
a bit saggy in the neck

well. what about this one?
i've told you before
i haven't got money to throw away
on rubbish

i don't like that kind of thing
looks terrible with your shoulders

you don't want that.
that's not what we're looking for.
you've several of those already.

what about this?
in another colour?
if they have it in your size.

i won't throw money away.
i've told you. no. no. no.
definitely not.
i don't care who else is wearing them

i can't understand
why you're so difficult
to please.

Jenny Boult

● Shopping

Close-up

❖ In pairs, read 'Granny in de Market Place' out loud.

Before you begin

• Make sure you know what the poem means. Some of the expressions may seem a little difficult at first.

• Try to get the feeling of the characters – Granny and the stallholders. How do they feel about each other?

• You will need to rehearse your reading a few times.

❖ The picture above shows a mother and daughter shopping. Could Jenny Boult's poem have been about two other people?

117

Poetry in practice

Response

Although both of these poems are apparently about shopping, the characters in them seem to interest the poets more than the goods on display.

- In groups of three, try using the poem 'Granny in de Market Place' to help you act out a scene in the market. Imagine that a policeman or woman has been called to the coconut stall where Granny is trying to break open a coconut to check that there is milk in it. One of the other stallholders has also come over, after watching Granny shopping for the last half hour. What might happen next?

- You may feel that the title 'shopping' does not fully explain what Jenny Boult goes on to describe in her poem. Can you think of a new title, one that describes what else is going on in the poem?

- Many people today feel they are pressurised into buying new clothes by the pictures in newspapers, magazines, on the television and at the cinema with which they are bombarded every day. Using pictures cut out from magazines, make a poster for Jenny Boult's poem. Choose a variety of images to bring out your view of what it is really about. You could use letters and words from magazines to make up the text of the poem.

The span of your mind

THE DOOR

Go and open the door.
   Maybe outside there's
   a tree, or a wood,
a garden,
or a magic city.

Go and open the door
   Maybe a dog's rummaging.
   Maybe you'll see a face,
or an eye,
or the picture
     of a picture.

Go and open the door.
   If there's a fog
   it will clear.

Go and open the door.
   Even if there's only
   the darkness ticking
   even if there's only
   a hollow wind,
   even if
      nothing
         is there,
go and open the door.

At least
there'll be
a draught.

Miroslav Holub (trans. Ian Milner and George Theiner)

Poetry in practice

Response

◆ Improvise a set of drama scenes based on this poem. You will need to:

- Reread the poem out loud.

- Imagine that you are going through a series of doors.

- Decide what you will find behind each one.

- React to what you find there and explore it further.

You may wish to use Miroslav Holub's suggestions about what lies behind the doors or to add your own ideas.

THE CALL

Come from your walls and your rooftops.
Come from your fires and lights.
Put on your cloak and let down your hair,
Come and walk with me tonight.

At the end of the asphalt roadway,
Walk out on the moor;
And I will show you the endless world
That you shut outside your door.

The moor is as wide as the span of your mind
And beyond that it goes on again –
With the grass and the scrub and the dark green gorse
And the sighing winds, and the rain.

Listen to the sound of the silence here,
Be still, and hear its song,
And the cares and the thoughts that imprisoned your mind
Blow away with the wind, and are gone.

Look out to the far horizon;
Look up to the boundless sky;
Oh, the world is wide, and wild, and we
Shall walk it, you and I.

Rachel Mueras

Response

❖ In groups, perform the poem to the other members of your class.

Before you begin

• Decide how you want to read the poem. You might like to have individuals reading a line, more than one line, or a verse each, or you could have more than one person reading at a time. Of course, you could alternate techniques as you go along.

• Rehearse the performance several times.

• Make sure that you understand the sense of the poem and that this shows in the way that you read it.

• Try to hear the music and rhythm of the poem.

The mysterious rider

Poems in Threes

THE WAY THROUGH THE WOODS

They shut the road through the woods
Seventy years ago.
Weather and rain have undone it again
And now you would never know
There was once a road through the woods
Before they planted the trees.
It is underneath the coppice and heath
And the thin anemones.
Only the keeper sees
That, where the ring dove broods
And the badgers roll at ease,
There was once a road through the woods.

Yet if you enter the woods
Of a summer evening late,
When the night-air cools on the trout-ringed pools
Where the otter whistles his mate,
(They fear not men in the woods,
Because they see so few.)
You will hear the beat of a horse's feet,
And the swish of a skirt in the dew,
Steadily cantering through
The misty solitudes
As though they perfectly knew
The old lost road through the woods
But there is no road through the woods.

Rudyard Kipling

THE LISTENERS

'Is there anybody there?' said the Traveller,
    Knocking on the moonlit door;
And his horse in the silence champed the grasses
    Of the forest's ferny floor;
And a bird flew up out of the turret,
    Above the Traveller's head:
    And he smote upon the door again a second time;
    'Is there anybody there?' he said.
But no one descended to the Traveller;
    No head from the leaf-fringed sill
Leaned over and looked into his grey eyes,
    Where he stood perplexed and still.
But only a host of phantom listeners
    That dwelt in the lone house then
Stood listening in the quiet of the moonlight
    To that voice from the world of men:
Stood thronging the faint moonbeams on the dark stair,
    That goes down to the empty hall,
Hearkening in an air stirred and shaken
    By the lonely Traveller's call.
And he felt in his heart their strangeness,
    Their stillness answering his cry,
While his horse moved, cropping the dark turf,
    'Neath the starred and leafy sky;
For he suddenly smote the door, even
    Louder, and lifted his head: –
'Tell them I came, and no one answered,
    That I kept my word,' he said.
Never the least stir made the listeners,
    Though every word he spake
Fell echoing through the shadowiness of the still house
    From the one man left awake:
Ay, they heard his foot upon the stirrup,
    And the sound of iron on stone,
And how the silence surged softly backward,
    When the plunging hoofs were gone.

Walter de la Mare

Poetry in practice

WINDY NIGHTS

Whenever the moon and stars are set,
   Whenever the wind is high,
All night long in the dark and wet,
   A man goes riding by.
Late in the night when the fires are out,
Why does he gallop and gallop about?

Whenever the trees are crying aloud,
   And ships are tossed at sea,
By, on the highway, low and loud,
   By at the gallop goes he.
By at the gallop he goes, and then
By he comes back at the gallop
   again.

R. L. Stevenson

Response

❖ All of these are story-poems, but each one tells only part of a story.
   Reread the poems. Choose your favourite and then write the whole of the story.

Before you begin

• Decide what happened before the beginning of the poem.

• Decide which characters to include and what they are doing.

• Decide how the story will end.

The mysterious rider

Poetry in practice

BYE NOW

    Walk good
        Walk good
Noh mek macca go juk yu
Or cow go buck yu.
Noh mek dog bite yu
Or hungry go ketch yu, yah!

Noh mek sunhot turn yu dry.
Noh mek rain soak yu.
Noh mek tief tief yu
Or stone go buck yu foot, yah!
    Walk good
        Walk good

GOODBYE NOW

    Walk well
        Walk well
Don't let thorns run in you
Or let a cow butt you.
Don't let a dog bite you
Or hunger catch you, hear!

Don't let sun's heat turn you dry.
Don't let rain soak you.
Don't let a thief rob you
Or a stone bump your foot, hear!
    Walk well
        Walk well

James Berry

Acknowledgements

The publishers would like to thank the following for giving permission to use copyright material in this book;

Cover, Bridgeman Art Library/Tate Gallery, London/ © Jasper Johns/DACS, London/VAGA, New York 1992; p29, Andes Press Agency; p30, Shahana Mirza; p36, Bruce Coleman Ltd; p42, Sally and Richard Greenhill; p44, Greenpeace Communications Picture Library; p59, Roderick Johnson/Images of India; p76, J Allan Cash Ltd; pp80–81, The Natural History Museum, London; p90, Topham Picture Source; p102, © The Guardian; p103, Reprinted by permission of the Peters Fraser & Dunlop Group Ltd; pp126–127, Sally and Richard Greenhill.

Irene Rawnsley for the poem 'Not Guilty'; Pan Macmillan Children's Books for the poems 'The Moth', Stephen Gardam and 'The Spider', Thea Smiley, both from *Young Words* (Macmillan, 1989); Jonathan Cape and the estate of W H Davies for 'The Fog', W H Davies; Scholastic Publications Ltd, for 'Long Distance Phone Call: Michael to Geraldine', Michael Rosen, from *The Hypnotiser* (Andre Deutsch, 1988); Amryl Johnson for the poem 'Granny in de Market Place', from *Tread Carefully in Paradise* (Cofa Press, 1991); Hamish Hamilton Children's Books for the poems 'Bye Now' and 'Goodbye Now', James Berry, from *When I Dance* © 1988 James Berry; The Literary Trustees of Walter de la Mare and The Society of Authors as their representative for the poem *The Listeners*, Walter de la Mare; John Johnson Ltd for the poem 'Warning', Jenny Joseph, from *Selected Poems*, published by Bloodaxe Books, © Jenny Joseph 1992; Shahana Mirza for the poems 'Two Worlds', 'Poetry', and 'Nobody's Fault', © Shahana Mirza.

Every effort has been made to trace and acknowledge ownership of copyright. The publishers will be glad to make suitable arrangements with any copyright holders whom it has not been possible to contact.